Clyde Hare's **Pittsburgh**

Photographs by Clyde Hare

Text by Alan Van Dine

PITTSBURGH HISTORY & LANDMARKS FOUNDATION

The photographer and editor are grateful to Bob Dougherty and Steve Plattner who gave advice and encouragement throughout the project; to Maria Zini, formerly of the Pennsylvania Department of The Carnegie Library of Pittsburgh, and Andy Anderson of the Ekstrom Library at the University of Louisville for providing access to and taking care of photographic collections of Clyde Hare's work; to C. Hax McCullough, Jr. for reviewing the text; to Marcia Rosenthal, fine arts consultant, for encouragement and marketing advice; and to Fran Esteban, Jeff Piatt, and the staff of BD&E, Inc. who so skillfully and generously supported the design of this book.

Photographs by Clyde Hare
Text by Alan Van Dine
Photographic notes by Walter C. Kidney
Project director and editor, Louise Sturgess
Graphic design by Jeff Piatt of BD&E, Inc.
Printed by The Stinehour Press, Lunenburg, Vermont
Typeset in Cochin and printed on 100 lb. Warren Lustro Gloss White text

Pittsburgh History & Landmarks Foundation
One Station Square, Suite 450
Pittsburgh, PA 15219-1170

Library of Congress Catalog Card Number: 94-67891
ISBN 0-916670-16-3

Contributors

Howard Heinz Endowment

The Revolving Fund for Education of the Pittsburgh History & Landmarks Foundation supported through major grants from the Claude Worthington Benedum Foundation, The Mary Hillman Jennings Foundation, and the Richard King Mellon Foundation.

Duquesne Light Company

Miles Inc.

National Intergroup

Westinghouse Electric Corporation

Clyde Hare's Pittsburgh

Four Decades of Pittsburgh, Frozen in Light

This is a book of moments worth capturing — encounters in the life and times of Pittsburgh, Pennsylvania, over a forty-year span stretching from the 1950s to the 1990s. It is, however, neither a city history nor a compilation of main events and principal buildings. That would be one kind of story; this is another. Everything here is seen through the lens, through the mind and the mind's eye, of a single and singular observer. The tradition is that of documentary photography. The result, snatched from the onrushing flood of people and things in motion, is a chronicle told in striking images with the power to bring it all back, alive.

Unlike the photojournalist who records a scene for the evening news or the next day's paper, the documentary photographer seeks out images with the power to convey the feel of this particular time, place, and cultural ferment to inhabitants of a different culture or a later generation. For Pittsburgh, just such a witness arrived in 1950, a turning point not only between halves of the twentieth century but also in the very life of the city and in that of its documentarist, Clyde "Red" Hare.

Continued on page 8

5

Clyde Hare's **Pittsburgh**

Continued from page 5

For this most American of cities, there is a "before" and an "after," and the year 1950 draws a line of demarcation between the two. This was the beginning of the urban transformation that would become known as the Pittsburgh Renaissance, as much of the central city was demolished to be rebuilt. It was the time when smoke control was clearing the skies, flood control was taming the rivers, the Pennsylvania Turnpike was linking the city east to west, and the Penn-Lincoln Parkway was connecting the turnpike with downtown Pittsburgh and downtown with its airport.

Until then, Pittsburgh was — in the words of those observers who weren't dumbstruck entirely — the *Valley of Decision, hell with the lid off, the smoky city* — the fiery furnace that had helped to forge the war effort but had become, in many eyes, a dark province of America where the skies were orange at night and gray by day. Now all of that was about to change.

And when the smoke lifted, there was Clyde Hare, with a camera of all things, and an eye — that and an almost uncanny sense of light, in a city where the light was returning for the first time in generations. Here was a young man from Bloomington, Indiana, who had never experienced the workings of a major city and who, like the city itself, would never be the same.

Growing up in Bloomington, Clyde had imagined many futures, none of which involved photography. As a child, he studied piano, picturing the life of a composer and conductor. In a high school project, he did a design analysis of the P-51 fighter plane, and his career plans shifted to aeronautical engineering. Later, he would consider a life in electronics, in marketing, or in management.

In the meantime, his mind churned with ideas brought to Bloomington by some of America's most original thinkers, writers, and artists. Clyde's mother was chief librarian of Indiana University's Kinsey Library, his grandmother a strong voice for a quarter of a century on the university's board of trustees. "As children of a highly visible trustee, we were expected to attend everything," he recalls. Aside from the plays, lectures, and concerts, there were opportunities to meet with the likes of Justice Learned Hand, Aldous and Julian Huxley, Gian-Carlo Menotti, and Amelia Earhart. It would have been hard to plan a boring life.

It was Mrs. Sanford Teter, Clyde's grandmother, who laid out the walkways for IU's mushrooming campus — not by drawing up plans but by waiting to see where students actually walked if no sidewalks were provided. Wherever a well-worn track appeared over the freshly sodded lawns, there was nature's choice of a pathway worth paving.

Photography? With the U.S. Navy in the final days of World War II, Clyde trained in radio and radar at Gulfport, Mississippi. At the naval hospital there, he taught patients how to use camera controls as a rehabilitation technique. His interest stirred. Reassigned to the Mare Island Naval Station in California, he crossed the country taking photographs as a travel record. But the real epiphany was still to come.

Back in Bloomington, now as a freshman marketing major, Clyde had a chance to enroll in the university's first course in photography as a fine art. The course was conducted by Henry Holmes Smith, who for many weeks would not let anyone in the class touch a camera. He talked about light, its tonal ranges and values, and had students fold paper in various ways and project light through it, studying the shadows, the highlights within shadows, the blackness of black, the whiteness of white.

Holmes had been an associate of Moholy-Nagy at the Art Institute of Chicago, which had become known as the Bauhaus West. For four years, Clyde absorbed not just the technique but the art of photography and the Bauhaus philosophy of design, beginning with the rediscovery of light itself. Photography was not about cameras or film or lenses or shutter speeds. Photography was about light. And all the while, materializing like the shadow of a future walkway across a green campus, his ultimate career path was becoming visible.

Clyde had freelance photos published in several national magazines, including assignments for John Morris of *Ladies' Home Journal*, one of the nation's leading authorities on photography. He also attended the first photographic workshop at the University of Missouri, where photojournalism was coming of age. Here, Clyde began a long association — first as student, then as faculty — with director Clif Edom and an ever-changing cadre of workshop leaders including some of the world's foremost photographers and photographic editors. It was at the Missouri workshop that he first met Roy Stryker, widely recognized as the father of documentary photography in America.

While still a student, Clyde was assembling a portfolio on college life in America. When he heard that Morris and Stryker were meeting to judge a regional photo competition in Milwaukee, he packed up four years of work and headed for Wisconsin, where he managed to get an appointment for a critique, hoping that he might also get some advice on what to do after graduation.

Clyde Hare's Pittsburgh

He got more than advice. The two men were struck by the documentary quality of Clyde's work, even at that early stage: real moments captured without a trace of contrivance. As Stryker had written, documentary photographers differ from pictorial or news or commercial photographers "chiefly in the degree and quality of their love for life. They insist that life as it is being lived daily, everywhere, in the streets, 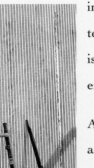 in the fields, the skyscrapers, the tenements, the hotels and huts, is so exciting that it needs no embellishment."

At Morris's suggestion, Stryker asked Clyde to join an unusual documentary project he was about to undertake — something called the Pittsburgh Photographic Library.

"There's Your City"

The idea was to catch history in the making. Pittsburgh was setting out to transform itself entirely: the city, the rivers, even the sky, which was destined to turn from gray to blue under heroic smoke control measures. Among the visionaries behind this enterprise, there were a few like Philip Broughton, Adolph Schmidt, and Edgar Kaufmann, Sr., who realized that here was an unprecedented opportunity to capture on film the metamorphosis of an American city. They enlisted the help of Park Martin, head of the Allegheny Conference, and Roy Stryker was asked to captain the effort from headquarters hastily set up at the University of Pittsburgh.

Under his direction, the Pittsburgh Photographic Library — known around the country as the Pittsburgh Project — mustered some of the nation's finest photographic talent. Esther Bubley, Russell Lee, and Richard Saunders were among the renowned photographers who accepted special assignments. Harold Corsini was technical director and Clyde Hare, along with Elliott Erwitt from New York, were the full-time staff photographers — the "kids" on the project.

When Clyde first arrived in a borrowed car, he got lost in the West End and stopped at a filling station for directions. There, he met a Pitt student who needed a lift to Oakland and offered to ride along and show the way. Cresting the top of McArdle Roadway — where downtown, North Side, South Side, the Hill, and all three rivers burst into panoramic view — Clyde's navigator signaled him to stop. "There's your city," he said.

Clyde returned later to photograph that sight (page 6). "It was my first real confrontation with a major city," he says, "and I knew it was mine."

It was also a work in progress. World War II was only five years past, the Depression only ten. The world was rebuilding on steel from Pittsburgh. Jones & Laughlin would light up the sky every night with spectacular pours at its new Open Hearth Number Four, landmarked by a mighty file of eleven stacks towering over South Side. Across the river, the first travelers to tunnel inbound under Squirrel Hill on the newly completed Penn-Lincoln Parkway confronted the hulking silhouette of the Eliza Furnaces. At the same time, as Clyde would later recall, "Downtown was in shambles. Everywhere you looked, something big was coming down or going up, and the earth shook from the piledriving."

Pittsburgh thought it was rebuilding to be a scrubbed-up Steel Capital of the World, this time with clean air and water and new highways. No one yet imagined that the real future was foreshadowed less by Jones & Laughlin than by Jonas Salk — that the incipient changes ran deeper than the pylons of Gateway Center and that healthcare, education, finance, communications, transportation, technology, and the arts would be the major industries where children and grandchildren of millworkers would chart their careers.

Either way, these were heady days, and Stryker was an extraordinary boss. A Colorado sheep herder, then an economist and Columbia professor, he had turned to photography in the thirties as the only way to make students realize the flesh and blood reality beneath the remorseless economic statistics of the Great Depression.

As chief of the Historical Section of the Farm Security Administration, Stryker had assembled a group of outstanding photographers — Walker Evans, Arthur Rothstein, Russell Lee, Dorothea Lange, and John Vachon among others — to document the marginal existence of rural America in the thirties. His idea was that of a permanent photographic file that would be open to the public. Through that vehicle, he achieved a visual document as compelling as John Steinbeck's literary portrayal in *Grapes of Wrath*, and Stryker reached a wider audience than Steinbeck, as FSA photographs haunted the pages of virtually every newspaper and magazine in the country.

Clyde Hare's **Pittsburgh**

In documenting the transformation of Pittsburgh, Stryker gave his photographers free rein. One went to live with a family in the Hill District for four months. Esther Bubley stayed in Children's Hospital.

Clyde Hare shadowed the demolition and reincarnation of the Point plus the life and times of some of the oldest sections of North Side and South Side, and the new stirrings of suburbia out in the hills.

When Stryker identified a subject that needed attention, he would call the team together. "Let's do transportation," he would say. One day he told Clyde, "Pittsburgh is a river city. We should do bridges. Now, Red, here are some of the things I think are interesting about bridges." Clyde left with his head swimming and nine pages of notes jammed into his pockets. The two became close friends and co-conspirators in the mission to define and defend the special responsibilities of documentary photography.

"**I** made up my mind to take one great photograph each day," Clyde remembers, "one that would live, would be simple, would have something to say."

Easier said than done, especially in documentary work, where the scene or the moment is to be discovered rather than staged. As Clyde puts it, "One of the things you try to do as a photographer is to remain a child. That first, wide-eyed look at something is what you want to get in your camera. And if you miss it, you know you've missed it."

In an interview with *Time* magazine in 1957, Stryker said of Clyde Hare, "He could have gone anywhere, but he fell for Pittsburgh and made up his mind to stay. His forte is structure, form, patterns, and their relationship to each other. And there is growing emotion in his pictures."

And what of his future? *Time* was interested, in part because by that time Clyde had been chosen by *Life* as one of the nation's most promising young photographers. "Red has great personal discipline and determination," said Stryker. "He'll do whatever he wants."

As a freelance photographer, Clyde was working in advertising, public relations, industrial photography, design, exhibits, video work, and lecturing — all areas where he is active today. He was also teaching at Carnegie Mellon University and was handling assignments for a number of national magazines, including *Life, National Geographic,* and *Fortune,* for whom he has shot fourteen cover stories.

When the Pittsburgh Project was complete, he teamed up again with Stryker, this time for an intensive seven years on the Jones & Laughlin Photographic File, taking pictures that have since been reprinted the world over, showing the glory days of big steelmaking. A number of the photographs taken for the J&L project and the Pittsburgh Photographic Library are included in this book.

Like any city, Pittsburgh bulges with accounts of its vital signs and its turning points: histories, studies, reports, analyses, newspaper files, statistical profiles of corporations, schools, hospitals, churches, teams, organizations, and governments. There is also the eloquent testimony of architecture, outlasting its impulse and standing ready to tell a story to those who can unravel it.

But to see the thing whole as experience, to see not only the changing face of the city but also the glint in the eyes and the stir of special moments, blessed or cursed, in the lives of people inhabiting those changes — to know in your heart how it was — that takes a special kind of record, one that seldom comes into being.

The occasional documentary project may rise to high excitement and be funded for a year or two or three, and its images may or may not be well preserved and catalogued. Quite aside from artistic powers, talents, and skills, one of the extraordinary things about Clyde Hare is the sheer persistence of his vision over time. With or without sponsorship, he has never stopped noticing, never stopped discovering and bringing back his discoveries on film. Always on the move, always with camera, he has quietly captured virtually every kind of experience that typifies Pittsburgh and its people since the time he first arrived.

Four decades of Pittsburgh, frozen in light.
There aren't many records like this anywhere…
of anything.

For historic and location details of each photograph, please see Photographic Notes, pages 157 through 164.

A City Rebuilding

"Downtown was in shambles.

Everywhere you looked, something big was

coming down or going up,

and the earth shook from the piledriving."

It was an odd yet fruitful collaboration: industrialist, general, philanthropist, thoroughly Republican financier Richard King Mellon and Democratic ward boss turned mayor David L. Lawrence. Their surprising alliance linked corporate and political action to keep the Pittsburgh Renaissance on track.

"It was a wonderful combination," recalls Clyde Hare, who spent days with each of these powerful men. "One of them knew everything that was going on in the clouds. The other knew all about what was happening in the streets."

And between the two of them, they had the power to move the earth — or enough of it, at any rate, to change the face of Pittsburgh in the early 1950s.

"One of them knew everything that was going on in the clouds...

...The other knew all about what was happening in the streets."

"A major change in the life of a city is

something that's visible to historians after it's over.

When you're in the midst of it, well…life goes on."

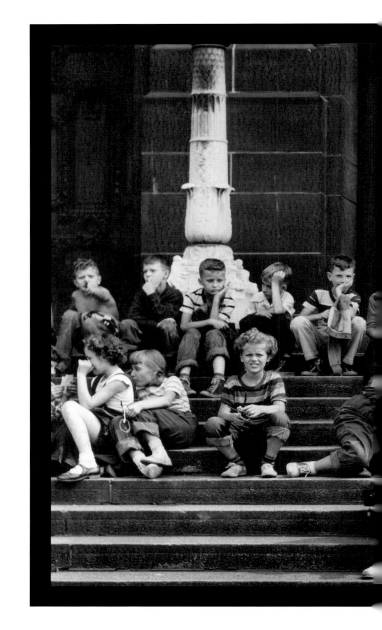

"It was the last Pe&LE steam train out of Pittsburgh.

When smoke control came in,

those old locomotives were fined $50 a minute,

all the way out to the county line."

A City At Work

"Pittsburgh knew what it was —

the biggest, mightiest steelmaker on earth."

The world had not seen — and will not see again — anything quite like the inferno of Big Steelmaking in the heyday of the open hearth and the blast furnace. Here, on a mythic scale, was hellfire without damnation.

The glory days survive mainly in pictures, and most definitively in the Jones & Laughlin Photographic File, now archived at the University of Louisville. Some of Clyde Hare's photographs from that documentary project are shown here. "This is the only way to understand the steel industry today," he says, "because it's gone."

"Against the massiveness of the mills,

the men seem tiny...

and yet you always know that these

are big, tough guys in complete control

of enormous forces."

"J&L's blast furnaces dominated

the parkway. When you entered

Pittsburgh from the east,

you were reminded what made

this city tick. At night, you might not

see the entire mill, but you saw

the fire in the sky."

t About Pittsburgh?

"It's the last place going east

where people still smile at you."

It keeps showing up on lists of the nation's most livable cities. It's certainly one of the least expensive and least intimidating. Everything downtown is in walking distance of everything else; and when you glance up you see the woods, climbing the bluffs across the river — across *three* rivers — so that Pittsburgh is also the greenest of cities, never estranged from its natural surroundings, and it's the bridge-buildingest town on earth.

Think of it as a small town with a couple of million extra people scattered about the hillsides — or a major city whose residents, for one reason or another, just never got around to getting cynical.

"People flock to the big spectator sports in town.

But going the other way, they can be out in the

country in 15 minutes; and in less than an hour

they can be hunting, fishing, sailing, skiing,

or backpacking."

"The cultural life of Pittsburgh is astounding.

We have years when the performing arts sell more

tickets than major league sports. But the real

story is what you see in people's eyes. Culture is

what people love to do — what they really want

to experience — when they're not at work."

"In most cities, transportation is two-dimensional.

Here, it's three-dimensional — tunneling through

hills, bridging the rivers, and sending inclines

up the slopes. And it's nature's flow, not man's:

When the river bends, so does the road or

the railroad."

"People here love to make things with their

hands — on the job, in the kitchen, in the garage.

Our workers have the skills to make everything

from pickles to robots to river barges, and then

the nuclear machinist goes home and makes

pierogies for the church picnic."

Made in Pittsburgh: Above left to right, pickles, bumpers, carbon steel, slag, chain-saw teeth, wire.

Below left to right, gear cutting, I-beams, mill rolls, aluminum foil, windshields, glass block.

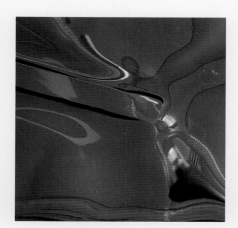

115

117

"I've worked with kids in various hospitals, and

in the School for the Blind, starting in the fifties.

I've cried shooting some of these photographs.

It's a bitter irony, using light to show what it's

like not to have any light at all."

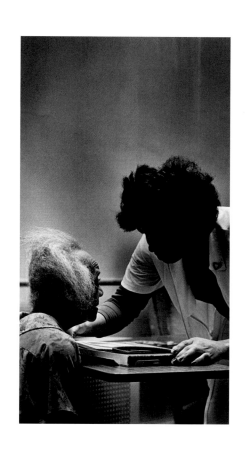

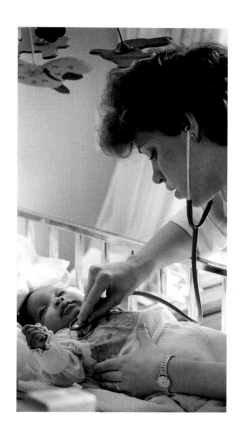

"I was raised on Carpenter's Gothic in the

Midwest — farm houses decked out in fancy

shutters and sashes and spindles, and all painted

white. The city is different, but the spirit is the

same. Our buildings express our pride and our

self respect. We've even managed to save some

of them for future generations to see."

124

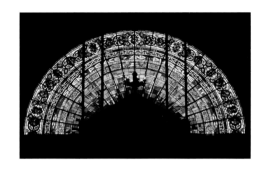

127

"Pittsburgh never lost touch with its natural

surroundings. For all of the changes we've made,

we're still crossing rivers between steep, wooded

hillsides, and we never get tired of looking at it."

"The hardest part of looking at the world around you is keeping your eyes and your interest as they were when you were a child — when all things were new, when every experience was a first experience, and your curiosity was insatiable. All you can add to that is a touch of aged patience and an awareness of relationships. What you try at all costs to resist is the veneer of sophistication and the weary habits of familiarity. Only the child knows: We see and live this only once, and it is forever different."

— Clyde Hare

Photographic Notes

These notes are based on the recollections of Clyde Hare and the knowledge of Walter C. Kidney, architectural historian of the Pittsburgh History & Landmarks Foundation. Many of the photographs in this book originally were taken for the Pittsburgh Photographic Library and the Jones & Laughlin Steel Corporation. The Pittsburgh Photographic Library project is now part of the collection of the Pennsylvania Department of The Carnegie Library of Pittsburgh. The J&L Steel Corporation collection is part of the photographic archives of the Ekstrom Library at the University of Louisville in Kentucky. Where a client is not specified, the picture was taken for the photographer's collection.

Page 6:
The Smoky City many of us remember, in its last days: a view of downtown from Mount Washington in 1950. The Wabash Bridge is already gone though one of its piers still stands to the right. The Pittsburgh Press Building, with its lighthouse-topped tower, is still free of its sheet-metal slipcover. To the rear, the units of Gateway Center are rising above recently-cleared land. Pittsburgh Photographic Library.

Page 7:
The Renaissance City at twilight, in 1989, from the McArdle Roadway Bridge on Mount Washington. The highest tower in this view is One PPG Place, whose pinnacles are illuminated. At its side is Fifth Avenue Place, with its unique split roof. Near the left side of the photograph is the Westinghouse Building (now Six Gateway Center), overlooking the Wabash Bridge pier, and farthest left are the lights of Three Rivers Stadium. In the foreground is the old Pittsburgh & Lake Erie Railroad Station, now The Landmarks Building and an element of Station Square, where adaptive use and new development are combined on a 50-acre site bordering the Monongahela River. In the 1950s the Pittsburgh Renaissance had little respect for the city's architectural past. The creation of the Pittsburgh History & Landmarks Foundation in 1964 marked the beginning of organized historic preservation in the city, and Station Square, a project initiated by Landmarks, has demonstrated what can be done.

Page 8:
Clyde Hare at 23, in 1950. Taken by George Cooper of the Pittsburgh Photographic Library staff.

Page 9:
Clyde Hare with his Linhoff in 1981, as taken by his wife Pat.

Page 10:
Clyde Hare at a construction site in the early 1980s.

Page 11:
Clyde Hare in Arsenal Park playground in 1987. Taken by his son Jerry.

Page 12:
Clyde Hare in 1991. Taken by Laurel Herman.

Pages 14/15:
Clearing the Gateway Center site downtown, near Liberty Avenue and Stanwix Street in 1951. Pittsburgh Photographic Library.

Page 16:
Richard King Mellon (1899-1970), whose power in the business and industrial community was essential to the Pittsburgh Renaissance of the 1950s. This portrait of 1962 was made in his office for *Fortune* magazine. "R. K. liked to sit and talk about photography" while subordinates paced outside his door, waiting to talk business.

Page 17:
David Leo Lawrence (1889-1966), politician and man of the people, collaborated with Richard King Mellon for the sake of Pittsburgh. Here is Lawrence in the Mayor's Office, spittoon at his side, photographed for *Time* magazine in 1957 in a rare moment of repose: "I was chasing him all day...never a harder guy to chase...always top speed."

Pages 18/19:
The city in 1950, from the West End Overlook. At the center, the former United States Steel Building on William Penn Way, now Three Mellon Bank Center, is being framed up. The Point Bridge of 1927 still crosses the Monongahela River, and the Manchester Bridge of 1913 still crosses the Allegheny River. In the foreground is the West End Bridge over the Ohio River. Pittsburgh Photographic Library.

Page 20:
Demolition of 218 Third Avenue, downtown, in 1951. Pittsburgh Photographic Library.

Page 21:
Building Two Gateway Center, about 20 floors up, in 1951. A foreman came to Clyde Hare, perched on another Gateway Center frame, and said that the ironworkers were being distracted waiting for him to drop off. He soon learned to "walk steel." Pittsburgh Photographic Library.

Pages 22/23:
As Gateway Center rises in 1951 the Pennsylvania Railroad freight terminal comes down, eventually to be replaced by Point State Park. A neatly-dressed man appears in a window, souvenir-hunting seemingly. To the right, the roof of Bouquet's Redoubt, the Fort Pitt Blockhouse of 1764, peeps above the ground. Pittsburgh Photographic Library.

Page 23:
The *Claudel Printz*, one of the last working sternwheelers, performs its regular task of shunting barges around the Pittsburgh area in 1951. At the far right, the last of the Exposition Buildings is under demolition, and in the center, Gateway Center is under construction. Pittsburgh Photographic Library.

Photographic Notes

Pages 24/25:

Children await the school bus, one day in 1952, that will take them home from a visit to the Carnegie Institute (now The Carnegie) in Oakland. The huge, diverse building was one of the few under-roof outing destinations for children. Pittsburgh Photographic Library.

Pages 26/27:

If not absolutely the last steam train in Pittsburgh, one of the last appears in this 1951 view at the foot of Mount Washington. The bright appearance of the smoke in the chance sunlight conceals its pollutive powers. Around this time, the City began to impose a $50-a-minute fine on locomotive smoke, and the railroads soon converted to diesel. Pittsburgh Photographic Library.

Page 28:

Early days on the Penn-Lincoln Parkway: a 1958 view near the Brady Street Bridge, alongside Oakland, with connections to Forbes Street and the Boulevard of the Allies.

Page 29:

Diamond and Stanwix Streets, downtown, in 1951. Streetcars have just passed beneath the arch of the Diamond Market, where Market Square is now. To the far right is the Wabash Terminal, demolished in 1955 to the ruin of three contractors. Pittsburgh Photographic Library.

Page 30:

The Oval in Schenley Park offers one of the city's most spectacular views. In this 1954 shot the camera looked out toward the South Side slopes.

Page 31:

A foggy day downtown in 1954, with the rare phenomenon of a scavenger's horse and wagon on the Smithfield Street Bridge over the Monongahela River.

Pages 32/33:

The Pennsylvania Railroad yards in the Strip District, in 1957, looking from the Herron Avenue Bridge toward Union Station on Liberty Avenue. In the middle distance is a coal tipple, surviving from the not-long-gone steam period, and beyond it the long diagonal of the Penn Incline, no longer running, which connected the Hill District with Seventeenth Street in the Strip District.

Pages 34/35:

A 1951 warm-weather scene at Sixth Avenue and Smithfield Street, downtown; placed in the past by streetcar tracks and the men's straw hats. Pittsburgh Photographic Library.

Pages 36/37:

Busy Liberty Avenue, downtown, in 1957: a telephoto shot from Ninth Street toward Gateway Center during late-afternoon rush-hour traffic.

Page 37:

A jaywalker at Penn Avenue and Stanwix Street in the heart of downtown, in 1977. Our city's outrageous jaywalking often becomes a high-speed dance.

Page 39:

A scene on Tustin Street, just west of the Brady Street Bridge, in the Bluff neighborhood that overlooks the Monongahela River east of downtown. Years after the 1952 picture, the little girl (then an adult) saw the picture in a show and asked Clyde Hare for a print; it was the only photograph of her mother. Pittsburgh Photographic Library.

Page 40:

This photograph shows a now-discontinued working practice; the casual throwing of tools is unlawful nowadays. A 1959 shot of a grocery under construction on lower Murray Avenue in Squirrel Hill.

Page 41:

Here is labor-intensive house painting, using brushes. Six painters finished this house, on Craig Street in Oakland, in one day in 1958.

Page 42:

Spring Hill as seen from Troy Hill on the North Side. The wooden "string bean" houses clinging to the hillsides are one of the most colorful and characteristic sights of Pittsburgh north and south of its rivers. Since 1951 and the taking of this photo, however, a significant number of the wood-frame houses shown have disappeared or gone to aluminum siding. Pittsburgh Photographic Library.

Page 43:

Leaving the school bus in 1952, in a raw suburb somewhere east of Wilkinsburg. Pittsburgh Photographic Library.

Page 44:

The most unusual lattice-truss structure of the IBM Building, downtown, was being framed up in 1962 when this was taken for *National Geographic Magazine.* (The building is now Five Gateway Center, the headquarters of the United Steelworkers of America.)

Page 45:

Walking steel on the bridge that was to carry the Pennsylvania Turnpike over the Allegheny River and on to Ohio. The riveter in this 1951 shot seems to like the exercise, since he is on the way to the very end of the truss to pick up fresh rivets. Pittsburgh Photographic Library.

Page 46:

A new cooling tower, under construction in 1973, for the pioneering nuclear power station at Shippingport in Beaver County. This was taken for a Duquesne Light Company advertisement.

Page 47:
The partly-opened dome of the Civic Arena, shown under construction in the lower Hill District area, around 1960. This structure, intended for the Civic Light Opera, appeared in *Fortune* as an illustration of Pittsburgh's Renaissance aspirations.

Page 48:
Building the Veterans' Bridge downtown over the Allegheny River in 1985. The mass of structure and machinery versus the tininess of men is a favorite Clyde Hare theme, and here a worker seems actually to be holding up a cantilever being positioned.

Page 49:
Here is another shot of the IBM Building's lattice frame under assembly in 1962, in the *National Geographic Magazine* series.

Pages 50/51:
Also for *National Geographic Magazine* in 1962 is this view of an approach of the Fort Duquesne Bridge under construction. The first hundred-ton beam used in U. S. highway construction is being lifted during a snowstorm. The Fort Duquesne Bridge crosses the Allegheny River near the Point.

Pages 52/53:
Open-hearth furnaces on Carson Street at the South Side Plant of Jones & Laughlin's Pittsburgh Works. Taken for the Pittsburgh Photographic Library in 1953.

Page 55:
A steamfitter foreman at the South Side Plant of Jones & Laughlin's Pittsburgh Works. This portrait, taken in 1956 for the United Steelworkers of America exhibit *These Are Our People,* shows a capable, exacting worker, not a man to tolerate sloppiness.

Page 56:
Again, the more casual safety attitude of the past, specifically 1956, photographed at the South Side Plant of Jones & Laughlin's Pittsburgh Works for the United Steelworkers of America. A man stands, one wooden-soled foot on a teeming platform and the other on the rim of an ingot mold into which steel has just been teemed. He is breaking up the crust of slag to keep gas from building up in the steel, accepting mortal danger as part of the job. "It was a wonderful period to see people at work."

Page 57:
This photo was taken on the Cleveland ore docks in 1958 for Jones & Laughlin Steel Corporation. A Hulett unloader, poised to take a bite of iron ore out of a boat hold, seems ready to swallow a workman.

Page 58:
A slag thimble car, again in 1958 and for Jones & Laughlin Steel Corporation.

Page 59:
This scene on the teeming platform at the South Side Plant of Jones & Laughlin's Pittsburgh Works shows protectively-coated men breaking the hardened tops on ingot molds. 1958, for Jones & Laughlin Steel Corporation.

Page 60:
A ladle charging a BOP (basic oxygen process) furnace at U.S. Steel's Edgar Thomson Works in Braddock, in 1984. The BOP furnace refines hot metal — freshly-smelted iron — with pure oxygen injected through a lance.

Page 61:
The open-hearth process dominated steel production for about a century. Here, in 1957, a workman at the South Side Plant of Jones & Laughlin's Pittsburgh Works has scooped up a shovel-ful of additives to fling into the steel bath of the open-hearth furnace from a safe 30 feet away, while a ladle charges the furnace with hot metal. Getting the additives through the small door from such a distance was one of the many challenges steelworkers had to meet. Photographed for Jones & Laughlin Steel Corporation.

Page 62:
The stacks of this open-hearth plant pollute the 1967 air, but the economic health is good. Busy stacks equal men safe and working: no shortage of orders, no accident to shut down a furnace.

Pages 62/63:
In the Second Avenue section of Jones & Laughlin's Pittsburgh Works. A solitary figure is steam-silhouetted while patroling an otherwise-deserted part of the plant in 1951. Pittsburgh Photographic Library.

Pages 64/65:
This 1953 view shows a bank of open-hearth furnaces still under construction on Carson Street at the South Side Plant of Jones & Laughlin's Pittsburgh Works. The building, with its mighty stacks, looks ready to stand forever, but the open-hearth furnaces lasted only a decade and a half, then were replaced by electric furnaces that operated about a decade more. Now, all traces of the giant construction are gone. Pittsburgh Photographic Library.

Page 66:
Here is an aerial photo of the Monongahela River Valley in 1963, with plumes of smoke coming from plants between the Homestead High Level Bridge and McKeesport. As far upriver as McKeesport, some 17 miles from downtown Pittsburgh, someone on the river usually had at least one major industrial plant in sight.

Photographic Notes

Page 67:
A view up the Monongahela River, taken from the Bluff in 1957. The now-gone Brady Street Bridge, from Soho to the South Side, is in the foreground. Further back, the Jones & Laughlin Hot Metal Bridge connects the Eliza blast furnaces on the north shore with the South Side Plant of Jones & Laughlin's Pittsburgh Works. The Works lined these shores for over two miles; the north shore was given over partly to the production of coke to fuel the adjacent blast furnaces whose still-molten iron — hot metal — was carried to the South Side Plant's Bessemer converters, open-hearth furnaces, or electric furnaces according to current practice. On the South Side, too, were most of the hot rolling mills, though some steel recrossed the river for strip rolling or cold finishing. All but the coke plant was closed by 1986, and most has now been demolished.

Pages 68/69:
The Penn-Lincoln Parkway is in partial use in 1956, though construction workers still have parking space to the right. Behind are Jones & Laughlin's six mighty Eliza Furnaces, successors to the first ones blown in in 1861. The parkway bore down on these in a most dramatic manner before turning to head into town. Ann, the last of the furnaces to operate, ceased production in 1979, and the furnaces and their accompanying hot-air stoves were all down by the end of 1983. Photographed for Jones & Laughlin Steel Corporation.

Page 70:
A misty morning in McKeesport, seen from a bluff across the Youghiogheny River near the point where it enters the Monongahela River. The year is 1955. The industrial haze in the atmosphere emphasized separation over distances, creating strong perspective effects.

Page 71:
The South Side flats and slopes, seen from the Boulevard of the Allies, about 150 feet above water level on the opposite side of the Monongahela River. The sheds at the South Side Plant of Jones & Laughlin's Pittsburgh Works dominate the flats, but the workers' houses dominate the hillsides in this scene of 1985.

Pages 72/73:
"Steel Cityscape" in 1977, shot westward through Jones & Laughlin Steel Corporation's Eliza Furnaces. Beyond the furnaces and smokestacks appear the skyscrapers of the Triangle. Tallest among them is the 841-foot U. S. Steel Building (now USX Tower), which has an exposed structure of Cor-Ten weathering steel. To its right is the 582-foot Gulf Building, tallest in the city until 1970.

Page 74:
A basic-oxygen furnace blow at Jones & Laughlin Steel Corporation's Aliquippa Works along the Ohio River, taken in 1960 for *Fortune*. The results of injecting pure oxygen into hot metal are awesome.

Page 75:
In 1965, a workman shields his face as he gas-dries a vessel. Heat and fire are the cleansing agents in a steel plant; water on its hot surfaces would explode.

Pages 76/77:
Industrial nocturne. Lights and flares reflect on the Monongahela River. Coke pushed from an oven catches fire and has to be quenched. A flare burning waste gas sends up a billowing, blossoming flame that makes an awesome termination to a Hazelwood street. The lights for the workmen are tiny breaks in the dark, but the great fires are seen for miles. "One thing Pittsburghers rarely experienced was the blackness of the night. If you lived close enough to the mill, that was your night light." This photo was taken in 1963.

Page 78:
A melter, in charge of an electric furnace, with the cobalt-blue glasses through which he inspects the steel being made. A photograph of 1965, for *Fortune*.

Page 79:
The main gate of U. S. Steel's Homestead Works (eight miles up the Monongahela River from downtown Pittsburgh), famous for its structural mill, notorious for the 1892 labor dispute. All this, photographed in 1964 for *National Geographic Magazine*, has disappeared.

Page 80:
A control stand at Jones & Laughlin's high-speed wire mill, at the Hazelwood end of the Pittsburgh Works. Rolling a white-hot billet into wire causes the steel to get thinner and thinner, longer and longer, and to travel faster and faster until it is passing through many rolls at once and going 100 miles an hour. The rolls have to be kept at just the right speed relative to one another or the glowing wire will break or, far worse, have a cobble, in which it crumples and goes dangerously in every direction as workers take cover. This photo is from 1962.

Page 81:
A coke push at the Hazelwood coke plant of Jones & Laughlin's Pittsburgh Works in 1959, when pollution controls were less strict. A ram at the back of the oven has sent the fresh coke into a basket-like quench car, which will carry it to a quench station to be doused.

Pages 82/83:
Breaking up slag in a newly-cast ingot from a teeming platform. Sparks of high-carbon steel seem to turn the air to fire. Photographed for *National Geographic Magazine* in 1961.

Pages 84/85:
Dawn breaks through the skeletons of new buildings, downtown, in 1982.

Page 87:
Pittsburgh Steeler fans waving their symbol, the Terrible Towel, at Three Rivers Stadium in 1978.

Page 88:
Night baseball at Forbes Field in Oakland: 1962. Forbes Field was demolished in 1970. Taken for *National Geographic Magazine.*

Pages 88/89:
A spur of the moment light-up downtown, in 1960, celebrating the World Series win by the Pittsburgh Pirates baseball team.

Page 90:
Nature near Pittsburgh: snowstorm in a woods in Allison Park, 1982.

Page 91, top:
Cornfield, pasture, and larches in north Butler County, 1982.

Page 91, bottom:
Heart's Content area of the Allegheny National Forest, north of Pittsburgh, 1978.

Page 92, left:
Fisherman by a foggy lake in Washington County, 1970.

Page 92, right:
A kind of moving sculpture: boys playing on the rim of the fountain in Point State Park, 1983.

Page 93, left:
Point State Park and Formula One tunnel boats in the Three Rivers Regatta of 1985.

Page 93, right:
Whitewater rafting on the Youghiogheny River near School House Rock at Ohiopyle, Fayette County, 1979.

Pages 94/95:
Wall-to-wall spectators at the Allegheny Wharf, Point State Park, during the Three Rivers Regatta of 1985.

Page 95:
Giant white trillium, *Trillium grandiflorum,* at the Fox Chapel Borough Flower and Wildlife Reserve in 1979.

Page 96:
Making up at the Pittsburgh Playhouse in Oakland, 1962.

Page 98, left:
Nathan Davis in concert at Hartwood Acres, playing the soprano saxophone, in 1983. Mr. Davis is director of Jazz Studies at the University of Pittsburgh.

Page 98, right:
High-school band at the Three Rivers Arts Festival in 1962.

Page 99:
In 1963, William Steinberg was music director of the Pittsburgh Symphony; here he talks with a harpist. Taken for *National Geographic Magazine.*

Pages 100 & 101:
Pianist Walter Klien, practicing in Heinz Hall for an evening performance of Stravinsky's "Concerto for Piano and Wind Instruments" in October 1983. "After covering guest conductor Leonard Slatkin's rehearsal, as I was starting to pack my cameras, Mr. Klien appeared from the wings and asked, Would it bother me if he practiced? I answered, No, certainly, and may I continue to photograph? He said, Yes, of course, and I was treated to what was, for me, one of my most wonderful emotional experiences, as I was favored with a private performance of beauty."

Page 102:
Downtown at the 1959 bicentennial of the creation of Pittsburgh, crowds pass along the Allegheny Wharf before the barge of the American Wind Symphony. In the background is the *Sprague* of 1902, largest towboat ever built, up from Vicksburg, Mississippi for the occasion.

Page 103, top:
A 1973 steeplechase at Rolling Rock Club in Westmoreland County.

Page 103, bottom:
The Pittsburgh Vintage Grand Prix, led by a Bugatti, in Schenley Park. Photographed in 1986 for Duquesne Light Company.

Pages 104/105:
The Monongahela Wharf and a passing tow, taken in 1957. Looking across the Monongahela River toward the old Pittsburgh & Lake Erie Railroad Station (now Station Square).

Page 106:
Winter in 1985: bridges over the Monongahela River. Front to rear, the Smithfield Street Bridge, Panhandle railroad bridge, and Liberty Bridge.

Page 107:
This photo was taken in 1984, the last whole year when the Smithfield Street Bridge carried streetcars.

Page 108:
Buses, pedestrians, and a boat: the Smithfield Street Bridge in 1982.

Page 109:
A view southward down the Penn-Lincoln Parkway in 1962, when the Eliza Furnaces were still startling apparitions at the turn of the road. Taken for *National Geographic Magazine.*

Photographic Notes

Pages 110/111:
Characteristic Pittsburgh: a woman making pierogies for a church festival, 1988.

Page 112, top left:
Making pickles: taken in 1980 for the H. J. Heinz Company.

Page 112, top middle:
Auto bumpers made by Rockwell International Corporation: taken in 1967 for *Fortune.*

Page 112, top right:
Carbon steel after grinding: 1982.

Page 112, bottom left:
A massive gear being ground at WHEMCO: taken in 1985 for WHEMCO (West Homestead Engineering and Machine Company).

Page 112, bottom middle:
First pass at rolling an I-beam: taken in 1972 for Jones & Laughlin Steel Corporation.

Page 112, bottom right:
The final test: a WHEMCO machinist runs his hand over a mill roll he has just turned. Taken in 1986 for WHEMCO.

Page 113, top left:
Slag on a blast-furnace casting floor: taken in 1962 for Jones & Laughlin Steel Corporation.

Page 113, top middle:
Sorting chain-saw teeth at Teneco in Beaver County: photographed in 1975 for Teneco.

Page 113, top right:
High-voltage electric transmission wire coming off an Alcoa weaving machine: taken in 1979 for Alcoa.

Page 113, bottom left:
Aluminum foil: taken in 1985 for Alcoa.

Page 113, bottom middle:
Racks of windshields, Pittsburgh Plate Glass Company (now PPG Industries, Inc.). Taken for *Fortune* in 1962.

Page 113, bottom right:
Contoured glass block by Ron Desmett and Kathleen Mulcahy for the upper level of the Steel Plaza subway station, downtown. Taken in 1985 for The Pittsburgh Cultural Trust.

Pages 114/115:
A coal miner coming off shift in 1969, probably at a Consolidation Coal mine; this photograph was taken for CONSOL Coal Group.

Page 116, top left:
Karen Crenshaw, an art conservator at the Carnegie Institute (now The Carnegie), with a binocular microscope: photographed in 1982 for Duquesne Light Company.

Page 116, top middle:
A steelworker inspecting a Jones & Laughlin blast furnace: taken in 1962 for *National Geographic Magazine.*

Page 116, top right:
A line of plate glass rouge polishers at PPG Industries' Creighton Plant: technology replaced by today's float glass process. Taken for *Fortune* in 1962.

Page 116, bottom left:
A construction worker on a housing project for Westinghouse Electric Corporation. Taken for Westinghouse Electric Corporation in 1972.

Page 116, bottom middle:
A laser scientist at II-VI Incorporated in Saxonburg: photographed in 1985 for the Pittsburgh High Technology Council.

Page 116, bottom right:
Orthopedic surgeon Dr. Michael Zernich of The Medical Center, Beaver, Pa., with a model of a hip replacement component: for *Connections* magazine, 1988.

Page 117, top left:
A machinist inspects a part of a large construction vehicle of the Anderson Equipment Company in Bridgeville: taken in 1983 for the Anderson Equipment Company.

Page 117, top middle:
Volunteer firemen, Hampton Township: 1977.

Page 117, top right:
A U. S. Steel experiment in magnetic-levitation melting for absolutely pure steel: the first such experiment made. Taken for *Fortune* in 1961.

Page 117, bottom left:
An experiment at the Cyclops Corporation in forging high-purity steel in an argon-filled chamber. Taken for *Fortune* in 1961.

Page 117, bottom middle:
Measuring a turned piece of steel 60 feet long and about 10 feet in diameter. Taken for WHEMCO in 1985.

Page 117, bottom right:
Dr. James Smith and Dr. Tae C. Min inspecting pathology slides at The Medical Center, Beaver, Pa.: for *Connections* magazine, 1988.

Pages 118/119:
"A young blind girl patiently awaits her turn for those few moments of attention that will form her knowledge of our world." Taken in 1951 at the Western Pennsylvania School for Blind Children in Oakland. Pittsburgh Photographic Library.

Page 120, left and middle:
At the Western Pennsylvania School for Blind Children in Oakland: teaching children to care for themselves. Taken in 1982 for the school.

Page 120, right:
Pediatric unit in The Western Pennsylvania Hospital in Bloomfield: taken for *Innerview* magazine in 1985.

Page 121, left and middle:
At the Lemington Home for the Aged in East Liberty. Taken in 1981 for The Pittsburgh Foundation.

Page 121, right:
Melanie Ericson, assistant head pediatric nurse at The Western Pennsylvania Hospital in Bloomfield. Taken for *Innerview* magazine in 1985.

Page 122:
At the Central Blood Bank, downtown: a child under treatment for hemophilia. Taken in 1982 for its annual report.

Page 123:
A girl at the Easter Seal Camp, wonderfully happy though burdened with disabilities. Taken in 1955 for the Easter Seal Society of Allegheny County.

Pages 124/125:
The Allegheny County Courthouse tower in shadow, against the tall buildings of Grant Street, downtown, in 1989. When built in 1888, the 310-foot Courthouse tower, a masterly work of H. H. Richardson, was the tallest construction between New York and Chicago.

Page 126, top left:
Mutual reflections of tower surfaces at One Oxford Centre, downtown: 1990.

Page 126, top middle:
A shop for produce from Spring Hill, close to the H. J. Heinz Company plant on the North Side. Taken for *National Geographic Magazine* in 1960.

Page 126, top right:
Stained glass over the main entrance of Rodef Shalom Congregation in Shadyside: photographed for the Pittsburgh History & Landmarks Foundation in 1989.

Page 126, bottom left:
A gable in the Mexican War Streets: photographed for the Pittsburgh History & Landmarks Foundation in 1984.

Page 126, bottom middle:
Detail of a Mid-Victorian house: 1990.

Page 126, bottom right:
Terra-cotta work on the Arrott Building, downtown: 1985.

Page 127, top left:
The pinnacles of One PPG Place, downtown: 1985.

Page 127, top middle:
First Avenue fronts, downtown, with the former IBM Building (now Five Gateway Center) in the background: 1980.

Page 127, top right:
Ceiling painting in the old Gayety Theater, now the Fulton Theater, downtown. Taken for The Pittsburgh Cultural Trust in 1986.

Page 127, bottom left:
Tracery over a doorway of the First Presbyterian Church, downtown: 1984.

Page 127, bottom middle:
Board ceiling of the Calvary United Methodist Church in Allegheny West. Taken for the Pittsburgh History & Landmarks Foundation in 1989.

Page 127, bottom right:
Brickwork at 200 Smithfield Street, downtown: 1985.

Page 128:
Freedom and restraint: a gateway at the Allegheny County Jail, downtown, taken in 1981.

Page 129:
The Allegheny County Jail and Courthouse, downtown, in a 1984 snowstorm.

Page 130:
Little League players on the North Side, in a 1962 picture for *National Geographic Magazine.*

Pages 130/131:
Valonia Street in the West End, 1989: a neighborhood of lived-on porches.

Page 132:
Liverpool Street in Manchester: taken for the Pittsburgh History & Landmarks Foundation in 1989 to show the recovery of a Victorian neighborhood.

Page 133:
A cover photo for *Innerview,* the magazine of The Western Pennsylvania Hospital in Bloomfield, 1985: house call on a porch in the Hill District by Dr. Edward Hale from the Home Care Department.

Pages 134/135:
Early morning in St. Michael's Cemetery in Knoxville, looking northwest toward downtown. Photographed in 1989.

Photographic Notes

Pages 136 & 137:
The demolition of a Pittsburgh landmark in 1990. St. Peter's Episcopal Church, built downtown in 1852, was the city's oldest and among its most distinguished, and had survived moving from the Triangle to Forbes and Craft Avenues in Oakland. But it was little used and deteriorating, and was sold to a developer. Under demolition, the outer wall in the right-hand picture collapsed all at once, to the surprise of everyone. The projected new building on the site was never started. Taken for the Pittsburgh History & Landmarks Foundation.

Pages 138 & 139:
These pictures were taken for The Pittsburgh Cultural Trust in 1987 to publicize the restoration of the Stanley Theatre downtown into the Benedum Center for the Performing Arts. After much frustrated maneuvering, Clyde Hare concluded that the bulbs inside the chandelier were off center and perfect symmetry was impossible.

Page 140:
The foyer of Heinz Hall, downtown, in 1989. Heinz Hall, like the Benedum Center, is a 1920s motion picture palace converted. Taken for the Howard Heinz Endowment in 1983.

Page 141:
Mellon Bank in the heart of downtown: a granite temple without, and a marble-lined hall 62 feet high within. Taken in 1983 for Mellon Bank.

Page 142:
This is a view of a fountain, downtown, installed in a new plaza beside Heinz Hall, donated in 1983 by the Heinz family. The fountain has dishes that tip and spill water, one into another. Taken for a presentation portfolio for the Allegheny Conference on Community Development.

Page 143:
A mother and son climb the inside steps and stop in the shadow-and-light world of The Carnegie Museum of Art, Scaife Wing, in Oakland, in 1983.

Page 144:
Public steps are one answer to Pittsburgh's 500-foot shifts of level. In 1962, jacketed students make the 150-foot climb from East Ohio Street to North Catholic High School on Troy Hill. Taken for *National Geographic Magazine.*

Page 145:
A stair and shadows on the Sixty-second Street Bridge, over the Allegheny River, 1988.

Page 146:
The Victorian wrought-iron gateway of the Calvary Episcopal Church rectory in Shadyside, 1956.

Page 147:
In memoriam: the Gwinner-Harter house, one of Shadyside's last great houses, burned out in 1986 just as its restoration was being completed. Taken in 1962 for *National Geographic Magazine.*

Pages 148/149:
Dawn breaks over the fog-shrouded city in this view of 1990.

Page 150, top:
The 680-foot tower of PPG Place, downtown, casts its shadow on low river fog at dawn in 1983.

Page 150, upper middle:
Here is another dawn view of the Golden Triangle from Mount Washington in 1989.

Page 150, lower middle:
Evening falls on the Golden Triangle in 1990.

Page 150, bottom:
A fall event is Light-up Night, when almost all the building lights are on downtown. The 1992 spectacle is seen here from Schenley Park Oval.

Page 151:
On a hazy morning in 1989, one of the 1877 cars of the Duquesne Incline climbs Mount Washington.

Pages 152/153:
Night approaches in 1993, and the city's lights come on while the setting sun continues to illuminate its towers.

Page 154:
In Schenley Park in 1953: Elizabeth Burgwin on the shoulders of Betty Burgwin.

Page 165:
H. J. Heinz II (1908-1987). Taken in April 1979 for the H. J. Heinz Company and the Heinz Family Collection.

In Appreciation

My thanks to my family for a natural curiosity and a sense of wonder toward all things; to Henry Holmes Smith for a relationship to art; to the University of Missouri Photojournalism Workshops and Clif Edom for showing me the potential of photography and truth; and most especially to Roy E. Stryker, director of America's great documentary projects, for his guidance, his wisdom, and his ability to make things happen.

It has been my good fortune through the years to work with great art directors, editors, writers, and photographers: Russell Lee, who had the positive, compassionate, and straight approach I so admired; Leo Leoni of *Fortune;* David and Hax McCullough; Bill Garrett of *National Geographic Magazine;* early on, Tom Ross of Ketchum MacLeod & Grove and his team of art directors including Frank Perry; Tom Morin and Eddie Byrd of the Westinghouse corporate design center; Laurel Herman in medical communications; the team at BD&E, whose Jeff Piatt is the designer of this book; Al Van Dine, who has had to straighten my convoluted sentences; Louise Sturgess of the Pittsburgh History & Landmarks

Foundation, whose always eager and energetic attitude is contagious; and to dozens of others who were challenged and excited by the potential of communicating through photographs.

Henry J. Heinz II

Till his death, I had a working relationship through photography with Henry J. Heinz II. Besides being a very good photographer, "Jack" Heinz appreciated the need to protect our photographic history and the permanent commitment required in the field of archival photographic preservation. I treasured our times together and will, with all the rest of Pittsburgh, miss his influence, taste, and dedication to things fine and right. He was the initial encouragement and support for the creation of this book. I hope some of his standards and desires have been met.

— *Clyde Hare*